How To W

Marketing

By

T.V. Wilson, Steve Branch and Thomas Hofler

To WANdA
See ya @ The
Top !!!

ISBN-13: 978-0-9819036-0-6 (pbk.)
ISBN-10: 0-9819036-0-6 (pbk.)
1. Selling 2. Business 3. Internet 4. Selling – Technological innovations.

Printed in the United States of America.

Table of Contents

Introduction

What is "relationship marketing"? This term has been used for decades to describe the power of selling products and services through the power of relationships. Recently, we have seen an increase in mainstream corporations; from banks to grocery stores use this concept to market to a consumer base while leveraging the relationships from person to person. Corporations reward referral sources through financial incentives to do business with their companies; while also turning the new customer into a referral source for additional potential sales leads. One example of this concept is the insurance agent who asks, "If you know of anyone looking for a good agent to meet their insurance needs, feel free to give me their contact information or have them to call me @..."A most recent example of this was when I saw an advertisement that a major bank was promoting for referred friends and family to its bank to open an account. The bank offered to pay the referring source a fee of $30 for the referral. Other companies offer relationship marketing incentives which include free service or products for a period of time in exchange for a referral that turns into a sale.

A major telecommunications company has a "circle of associates" plan that gives savings for callers within "your network"; which basically means a discount on calls made to those who you refer to their company and eventually become customers. Major

1

brands in the travel industry, healthcare industry and just about every other industry in between understand that relationship marketing is a powerful tool to build revenues for their companies with the lowest cost possible. The bottom line is that relationship marketing is here to stay and this method of marketing is expected to explode over the next few years to come.

We have written this book to educate and provide some understanding about the power of relationship marketing and what it can mean to the average person who is looking to start their own company to generate some additional income or those looking to work part time to earn extra money. We also want small and major corporations to understand the power of using this form of marketing to build a strong competitive position in your various markets and increasing your revenues, while saving on the cost of marketing your corporation using traditional forms of advertising. The information contained in the pages of this book have come from decades of entrepreneurial experiences of three successful business men who have made millions in their own companies over the years, while having gone through the tough times that every entrepreneur will eventually experience.

Relationship marketing is here to stay and has been here in many forms as a proven business system since the 1940's. The Direct Selling Association, a leading national trade association has forecasted that by 2010, the industry will produce over $700 billion in revenue. Major brand name corporations use a form of this type of marketing to sell billions of dollars in products and services every year. Simply put, the business of selling goods and services through a network of people by referral is a low cost, high leveraging value proposition for corporations looking to sell these goods and services as well as those looking to profit from building a network to aid these corporations in that endeavor.

So, let's jump into the information and resources that will help you to better understand this exciting and growing industry that has changed the bottom line of many major corporations while providing a powerful financial opportunity and change of lifestyle for many people around the world.

Part One: Understanding the

Facts about Relationship

Marketing

Chapter 1:

Forms of Relationship Marketing

There are several forms of relationship marketing that we would like to define and provide some additional understanding. We realize that various people who have been in this industry for any substantial length of time have seen their share of new labels on an old concept. We have seen the industry grow and mature over the years and we hope to give you our perspective on relationship marketing and the various forms within this great industry that has been around for over 40 years.

Direct Sales

What is today known as the Direct Selling Association (DSA) was formed in Binghamton, New York in 1910. When it was founded, the association was called the Agents Credit Association. The formation of this organization marks the start of the modern-day direct selling era. In 1900, there were less than 93,000 traveling salesman. There was a need, based on the growing numbers, to form a national association - one that would look after the needs of direct selling companies and create an image for direct selling as a respectable profession. This would be done by making sure that ethical business methods were observed.

The DSA is the national trade association of the leading firms that manufacture and distribute goods and services sold directly to consumers. More than 200 companies are members of the association, including many well-known major brand names. Today, the DSA operates from its D.C. headquarters. It shares offices with the Direct Selling Education Foundation and the secretariat of the World Federation of Direct Selling Associations. DSA provides educational opportunities for direct selling professionals, works with Congress, numerous government agencies, consumer protection organizations and others on behalf of its member companies.

The DSA's mission is "To protect, serve and promote the effectiveness of member companies and the independent business people they represent. To ensure that the marketing by member companies of products and/or the direct sales opportunity is conducted with the highest level of business ethics and service to consumers."

At the foundation of the DSA's commitment to ethical business practices and consumer service is its Code of Ethics. Every member company must pledge to conduct its business by the Code's standards and procedures as a condition of admission and continuing membership in the DSA. To gain membership to this organization companies must meet this standard. For more information on this organization and its Code of Ethics visit: www.dsa.org.

Direct sales are quickly becoming the small business option and work from home job of choice of the 21st Century. Though they are mostly known in times past for home parties, many companies who choose this method of relationship marketing have many alternate ways to sell their products, which will be discussed in later chapters.

It is quickly capturing the attention of companies struggling to compete in the world economy. Because of the many new products that are being delivered by this marketing model, consumers are adjusting to the concept of being introduced to new products in this manner. Direct sales offer a great way for everyday people to get into business for themselves. While some are free, some cost only a small amount to start. Direct Sales is a very rewarding home based business choice. It offers you a relatively structured business model with a proven record of success. Direct sales are expected to gain a stronger presence in the United States and around the world.

Starting a direct-selling business and building a team not only means the potential to make good money, but it also builds invaluable leadership skills that many people can leverage into corporate careers. This is a way for anyone who wants to be at home to control their income while making money and building professional skills. Start up kits can range anywhere from $5 to $800 and up based on the company. If you don't need to purchase a start up kit, it is highly advised that you do so to educate yourself on proven business systems that the company has taken time to develop for your success.

Referral Marketing and Viral Marketing

Referral marketing is the art of getting people, who may not even be your customers, to refer your product or service to other people, typically their friends or acquaintances. Viral marketing, simply put, is referral marketing over the Internet. Referral marketing is a better deal for all of us, and it is a legitimate form of conducting business.

Referral marketing is the most cost-effective way of attracting new clients. Generating prospects from targeted advertising, direct mail, telephone calls, and other methods have their own level of effectiveness. Referral marketing is being increasingly used in marketing of services, like education. As more and more foreign universities are trying to recruit students of Indian and Asian origin to pursue courses offered by them, referral marketing may be an innovative tool to use for their marketing efforts. Referral marketing is all about cultivating a good relationship with your prospects and clients. The better you are at developing a relationship with them, the more your business will grow.

Referral marketing is an extremely cost-effective way to market and is the ultimate equal opportunity platform, which in part explains its obvious success. It is our free enterprise system in its purest form. Referral marketing is based on developing relationships with others, business or marketers who have an existing relationship with potential clients, i.e. a close cousin to referral marketing is word of mouth marketing, which tends to be driven by satisfied customers sharing company names with their friends, family, coworkers and acquaintances.

Referral Marketing is a unique skill and takes a lot of hard work. Like any form of marketing, it involved a "On the Top of Mind Awareness" system to make sure you or your company are not forgotten. Referral marketing is one of the most ethical business models we've ever seen. It builds and develops people in a massively positive way when the right business systems are in place. Referral marketing is the most powerful method for generating new customers. The most successful entrepreneurs will tell you: no other method of marketing produces more leads, customers and sales than referral marketing can. There is nothing like a successful referral marketing campaign to give you the competitive edge.

A referral marketing strategy is perhaps the most effective marketing strategy in today's competitive environment; but it requires thorough long term planning. Here are some tips for streamlining your referral marketing strategy. The first thing you need is patience; unlike most other marketing strategies, referral marketing needs a slow and steady pace. Second, listen and learn about the interests that you share with your referral sources and instead of attending stiff lunches or cocktail parties, go boating, running or golfing with them. Do what you enjoy and invite others to do the same. Marketers should experiment with different tactics.

Referral marketing has many different techniques. I remember years ago when I was building a successful healthcare company going to various Doctor's offices handing out donuts and coffee in the morning. This was met with extreme delight by the office workers who then thought about us when it was time to refer patients and clients to our company. Use your imagination and think about what you would want someone to do for you that would cause you to remember them.

Referral marketing (also known as viral marketing) is a high tech way of getting your visitors to tell other people about your site. The term viral marketing was coined by venture capitalist Steve Jurvetson in 1997. He used the term to explain the exclusive referral-marketing program produced by Hotmail, one of the primary free e-mail services. Several outsourcing companies around the world are providing viral marketing services for companies who are interested in using this method. With viral marketing, a company's products or services are spread "virally," or from person-to-person-to-person in a long chain throughout the Internet. We've all known someone (or even ourselves) who may have gotten a cold, only to spread it to someone else. This is the concept of viral marketing.

Most referral marketing is by word of mouth or other advertising methods, but this could help to generate some extra interest in your site. As a referral marketer you should become involved in at least three different kinds of organizations. These usually, but not always, include a strong-contact network such as a trade association, a casual-contact network such as a chamber of commerce, and a charitable or service organization like the Kiwanis or Rotary.

Referral marketing is also very cost-effective, much cheaper than traditional advertising. These reasons explain why referral marketing is the most popular marketing strategy for accountants, lawyers, insurance agents, real estate agents, and most people in the service industry. Referral marketing helps to motivate current and former clients and other professionals to refer others to your organization. One can prospect a referral once they have been referred to your business. Prospecting is communicating directly with potential clients to make them aware of your company and to encourage them to retain your services or buy your products. Referrals are the cheapest and most effective marketing there is, and they tend to bring the best types of clients and customers.

Affiliate Marketing

Affiliate marketing is a way that Internet businesses can market their products and services at a minimal cost. This is done by creating several click through ads, showing their products or services that will redirect anyone who clicks on them back to that business's web site. Affiliate marketing is an awesome opportunity for those who are self-motivated. If you brand your affiliate program as the best out there for your industry it could yield tremendous results. Affiliate Marketing is about developing profitable, strategic and long-term win-win relationships.

It is an online advertising channel for which advertisers pay only for results. These results might be either a visitor filling out a form on their website or purchasing a product or service. This method of marketing is a great way to sell products online or selling other company's products online through an agreement between a merchant and a website owner. The website owner, or the affiliate, allows the use of their site for the promotion of the merchant's products by linking to the merchant's website. Affiliate marketing is considered a revenue sharing between a merchant and an affiliate who gets paid for referring or promoting the merchants products or services. It is one of the burgeoning industries online now because it has proven to be cost-efficient and a quantifiable means of attaining great profit both for the merchant and the affiliate and the other players in the affiliate program, such as the affiliate network or affiliate solution provider.

For these reasons, many companies (especially those that started in the early days of e-commerce) owe a tremendous amount of gratitude to the concept of affiliate marketing (amazon.com is a good example). It has now become normal for companies to include affiliate marketing in many of their marketing plans. Affiliate marketing is also a cost-effective way of building online sales by having other companies send customers to your site. The main issue to overcome with this type of marketing is having the proper software to track affiliate sales. Affiliate marketing is a very cost effective solution because it allows you to base advertising on a pay-per-performance model. Instead of paying for advertising, merchants using affiliate marketing programs pay only when advertising results in an actual sale. Web merchants have two basic methods for providing an incentive to website publishers to promote the offer: Cost per action and revenue sharing. WebSponsors for example, will pay you when someone requests a free trial or sample of a product or service. You provide them with a lead and they pay you for it.

From a merchant standpoint, the Return on Investment (ROI) for affiliate marketing is much greater as merchants pay only for results. Merchants can request that affiliates do not merely send them traffic, but send them qualified traffic that takes action on their site. This means that merchants are paying for traffic that shops around and has a real interest in the products and services offered on their site.

Affiliate marketing is a new concept for many people. However, the simple idea is to hire and train a sales force that you don't have to pay until they make a sale. It is effective and you don't have to deal with the product creation and shipping if you are the one joining an established affiliate marketing program. Affiliate marketing is the original and purest form of performance-based media and a critical weapon in the customer acquisition arsenal for many online sellers. Affiliate publishers can deliver a steady stream of online sales and prospects in exchange for a commission, but affiliate marketing does not equate to the concept of "build it and they will come". Affiliate marketing is not easy work but it's definitely a good way to build a side business that could have the potential to be a lucrative endeavor. Affiliate marketing is flourishing and spreading across the internet at a rapid rate. Some would argue that the future for Affiliate Marketing is as far reaching as that of the internet itself.

Affiliate marketing is a robust channel that can't be ignored, especially as part of a multi-channel marketing strategy. It is certainly an art in one since, but don't be fooled, there is a science behind the data that can be mined from the buying habits of consumers. One way to gain some insight if you are new to this form of marketing is to discover the top affiliates for any program and copy what they are doing. I once read that copying is the best form of flattery. Nevertheless, as the old saying goes, "if it isn't broke, don't fix it".

Affiliate marketing is all too often overlooked when considering a marketing budget to invest your advertising dollars. While advertising in general is best diversified, using an affiliate marketing strategy should always be a part of your overall marketing plan. Unlike other forms of advertising, with an affiliate program, you pay only for performance as the seller of products and services. Affiliate marketing isn't just for newcomers to the internet marketing game, it isn't just for people too small to make a difference in the world and it isn't just for people unable to create their own products. However, if you are more advanced in your internet marketing journey, starting your own affiliate marketing business is also a possibility; this however will involve more effort on your part and a greater time investment from you. Either way, affiliate marketing can be a relatively simple, yet rewarding opportunity for both sellers and those looking to earn income from participating in these programs.

Multi-Level Marketing

Over the years the term Multi-Level Marketing has taken a beating in mainstream media and among those who refer to this system of marketing as "one of those things". Multi-Level Marketing (MLM) takes advantage of the greatest form of advertising, "Word of Mouth". Unfortunately, it is in the sometimes execution and hype behind this form of marketing that causes problems. Some unwise persons involved in these activities give the term MLM a bad name in the eyes of mainstream business and the public in general. There are always people who ultimately act unethical that can taint an otherwise great marketing approach. These people typically don't understand basic business principles that are required to run a long term successful enterprise. With that said, let me take time to share with you a proven powerful marketing system that has great potential for selling massive products and services while empowering average people with a vehicle that can have tremendous financial rewards.

Multi-level marketing is a system where people make money by getting other people to become "distributors" for a product. While some money may be made by actually selling the product, most money is made by creating layers and layers of people who are distributors working under your main distributorship. Multi-level marketing is a lawful and legitimate business method that uses a network of independent distributors to sell consumer products. On the other hand pyramid schemes take on a line of products and claim to be in the business of selling them to consumers in order to look like a multi-level marketing company (more about this in the next chapter). Multi-level marketing was the biggest growth industry in the 1980's. It has been termed as the last true rags-to-riches opportunity left in North America, and its ability to bring enormous incomes to common everyday people who work at it is legend.

MLM's are similar to affiliate marketing programs. It is also an excellent source of earning over the internet and running business from home. MLM is an offshoot of direct selling in that the salesman buys from the company wholesale and sells at the higher retail rate to the customer. However, in MLM you have the added efforts of other salesmen working with you and thereby leverage the efforts of others.

This is a popular and legal way of retailing. Consumer products are sold - not in stores by sales clerks - but usually in customer's homes by independent businessmen and women (distributors). MLM is very attractive because it offers the opportunity to earn income and gain independence for a relatively small up front cost. The product or service can be a new and revolutionary medical break through offered no where else, or even an established product offering like cosmetics.

When participating in a MLM program it is basically a partnership with others for the long term. It is when you go into business with someone who has the same interests and business goals that you have. It is not a get rich quick scheme like some would like you to believe. It is like any other business endeavor; and what you put into it will yield you a corresponding return. The multilevel marketing concept is based on the premise that if a person signs up to sell a company's products, the company will pay you a commission on all sales generated by that person, as well as the additional products or services that person's team may sell. A note of caution here, any company that pays you to recruit people only should be carefully considered before you get involved. Selling products, services or franchises is the primary way that one should make income, gain commissions or earn bonuses.

For example, if a company is selling a business that will provide a distributor access to a web site where certain products or services are sold and there is a licensing fee that is charged to the distributor that one can make a commission for selling, then this is a legitimate form of earnings. Your income in any MLM should not be dependent on signing up new people and collecting their sign up fees. It is true that as you sponsor more distributors you increase the potential to leverage the efforts of others to earn more money. This is no different than any major corporation or traditional business. The more people they have working for the company the more there is the potential to earn income from their efforts. However, in the MLM opportunity example we are using here, there should be provisions with that company that give anyone the opportunity to join the company without paying a fee.

Multi level marketing itself is NOT a scam, the Federal Trade Commission only considers a company to be scandalous if they promote a "pyramid scheme" designed with the sole purpose of promoting a pyramid and nothing else. We are in no way legal experts so seek the advice of legal counsel if you have a question about whether a company is following the law in your state.

With MLM companies you will always hear people talk about duplication, but that is not always easy to do. For example, you can't duplicate a person's charisma, leadership skills or personality. There could be a prospect who hears about a MLM opportunity from one person and for whatever reason decided to decline from participating in the business opportunity. Only later to talk to someone else with whom they feel more comfortable. I have gone to a McDonald's restaurant in one part of town and did not return because of poor service and yet, it did not affect my desire to go to another one on the other side of town that I liked. Both are McDonald's restaurants but I choose to do business with companies and people that I prefer. I am sure that you are the same. It all comes down to what we have covered in previous chapters. What value do you bring to the opportunity?

MLM businesses operate in the United States in all 50 states and in more than 100 other countries around the world. It is a legitimate method of business which removes traditional methods of marketing, and puts people like you and me in the driver's seat. When done right you can become associates of a proven company with a proven product. MLM is a career and one must be prepared to give it what it takes to succeed like any other business.

Network Marketing

Network Marketing is a cousin to the MLM. A large difference between the two is in the pay structure or set up of the marketing system. Network Marketing is a proven business system in its own right. Income is generated in two ways - through personal sales and bonuses earned from team building. Network Marketing is the actual sale of products, services, or information to others within a cohesive and strongly built team environment. To break it down simply, however, Network Marketing is a process in which you share information while developing contacts. Network marketing is not recommended for everybody as it requires an investment in the building and development of people over the long term.

Network marketing is considered the fastest growing home-based business opportunity in the country. The Direct Selling Association forecasts that by 2010, network marketing companies will produce over $700 billion in revenue. Network marketing is a branch of the direct sales industry that has been around for over 40 years. As it has evolved today, network marketing is one of the rare options whereby people can leverage themselves by duplicating their efforts through their relationships with other people. Network marketing is an awesome way to build a strong financial future over time. If you're working, you could use your income from your job to invest into a home based network marketing business.

As long as you trade time for money, you will be hard pressed to have financial security or the abundance to have a lifestyle that most people dream about. It's an affordable option for anyone with a desire to have their own business that can produce a comfortable income, and create the lifestyle and freedom they want. Network marketing is a powerful business concept for many reasons but the most obvious is for the type of income it can provide the network marketer. It is so powerful that many fortune 500 companies have used, some are still using, this business model to build their multi-million dollar empires.

Many network marketing companies use computer software on your desk top or online that help you in marketing your business with back office technology to keep track of you and your team's sales activities. Typically network marketing companies provided accounting and other services that help you stay focused on driving sales. In an online network marketing affiliate program, the products marketed are those that the website sponsoring the network marketing business have available. Network Marketing has really gone high tech even though it has been traditionally based on person-to-person contact by sharing product samples and information. While hard selling is not involved, follow-up is required.

Although technology is being used now in building successful network marketing businesses, no amount of technology can replace the basic philosophy of the network marketing business model. That philosophy simply put, is that network marketing is about the relationship that you develop with your clients and your team members. One thing you should realize is that the glue that will hold your network marketing business together is your ability to communicate, interact and mentor your team members. Network marketing has the ability to educate and support the marketing and sales process, in order to facilitate an educated product purchase. Networking marketing is more about farming than it is about hunting. This means you need time to cultivate the contacts you make. Network marketing is the ordinary person's best opportunity to make extraordinary income. Well known author of the famed book series Rich Dad, Poor Dad, Robert Kiyosaki, says that "most ethical network marketing businesses are like business schools". One can learn to develop long term successful business skills by working in the structured system of a good network marketing business. Network marketing is truly a win-win type of business.

Chapter 2:

Avoid Ponzi Schemes, Illegal Pyramids and Other "Lions, Tigers and Bears"

We have included this chapter as a way to educate our readers on the dangers of participating, knowingly or unknowingly, in illegal scams that have the potential to not only cause you to loose your hard earned money but could also drag you into serious legal trouble. As we have traveled the world, we have found many people who have questions about ponzi schemes, illegal pyramids and other types of scams, that we felt a need to try to provide some insight based on the research we have done on these subjects. This chapter is only for the purpose of introducing some basic concepts, and we highly advise you to consult with a competent attorney who has expertise in these areas if you have a desire to get more information.

The term "Ponzi" scheme is named after Charles Ponzi, an Italian immigrant, who became notorious for using the technique in the United States. Ponzi promised investors 50% returns in 45 days on an investment of $1000 in postal coupons. He raked in millions of dollars in investments in less than a year in 1920. Ponzi was not the first to invent such a scheme, but his operation took in so much money that it was the first to become known throughout the United States.

Today's schemes are often considerably more sophisticated than Ponzi's, although the underlying formula is quite similar and the principle behind every Ponzi scheme is to exploit unsuspecting investors. A Ponzi scheme usually offers abnormally high short-term returns in order to entice new investors. The high returns that a Ponzi scheme advertises (and pays) require an ever-increasing flow of money from investors in order to keep the scheme going. The system is doomed to collapse because there are no underlying earnings from the money received by the promoter. In short, typically no product or service is sold.

However, the scheme is often interrupted by legal authorities before it collapses, because a Ponzi scheme is suspected and/or because the promoter is selling unregistered securities. As more investors become involved, the likelihood of the scheme coming to the attention of authorities increases.

Another form of fraud similar in some ways to a Ponzi scheme is called a pyramid scheme. It relies on a disbelief in financial reality, including the hope of an extremely high rate of return. However, there are several characteristics that distinguish pyramid schemes from Ponzi schemes. Namely, in a Ponzi scheme, the schemer acts as a "hub" for the victims, interacting with all of them directly and therefore benefits solely. In a pyramid scheme a team of those who recruit additional participants benefit directly. In fact, failure to recruit typically means no investment return. Furthermore, a Ponzi scheme claims to rely on some esoteric investment approach, insider connections, etc., and often attracts well-to-do investors; pyramid schemes explicitly claim that new money will be the source of payout for the initial investments. A pyramid scheme is bound to collapse a lot faster, simply because of the demand for exponential increases in participants to sustain it. By contrast, Ponzi schemes can survive simply by getting most participants to "reinvest" their money, with a relatively small number of new participants. Pyramid scheme participants gain money by attracting others to the scheme. Ponzi scheme participants gain their money by increasing their investment and hopefully their share of the profits from the successful development of the scheme. A scam artist may pay money out of their own pockets in order to convince an investor to give them more access to their money.

Ponzi or Pyramid "investment" schemes have been qualified under federal law as "dependent in whole or in part upon on lot or chance". The very nature of these schemes is one based upon a small number of people profiting before the scheme collapses, thus "dependent in whole or in part upon lot or chance". In short, these scams and other similar scams can be the cause of major financial ruin as well as legal problems, even if one unknowingly participates. Avoid the drama!

Part Two:

Old School Still in Session

Chapter 3:
Developing a Millionaire Mindset "Did You See The Movie?"

Over the 22 plus years I have been involved relationship marketing I've have learned that if you are going to make significant amounts of money in business you must have a millionaire mindset. Success in business starts with the mind set of the individual wanting to become wealthy in a worthy endeavor. Many of the millionaire mentors I have had over the years taught me that one must be willing to learn from those who have accomplished what one desires to accomplish. To do that one must be willing to trade ego for equity. As a part of this process, we must be willing to reprogram our thinking because most of us have been programmed through over 14,000 hours of formal school education in Math, Social Studies and English from grade level to grade level. This teaching primarily programmed us to think that all we needed to do to be successful in life financially was to make good grades, get a good job and start at the bottom of someone's corporation. And if we work hard one day we will make it to the top of the corporate ladder of success. Yeah Right.

How many people do you know that started out at the bottom of the corporation in the same company and was promoted to middle management and eventually was promoted to the Executive Suite and became the President and CEO of that same company? I'll give you a minute... You are probably like me and after all of these years asking tens of thousands of people around the world this same question, I have yet to have anyone to name one person. So I'll give you another minute... OK, not relatives with the same last name, a college fraternity brother nor the guy that hangs out at the country club with them. And unless this is the case, you probably won't even become a VP in the company. We need to change the VP acronym in the company from Vice President to Very Personal friends and family members.

This is fundamentally the reason why most middle managers are at the greatest risk of being adversely affected by what I call being "involuntarily separated from payroll" or otherwise, corporate down sizing and layoffs. By keeping their friends and family members in place, keeping low wage workers or outsourcing the same to temps, top management is able to take the excess cash flow gained by eliminating middle management and use the excess money to pad their pockets, fly around in their private jets and take vacations at your expense. Ask yourself who really gets to make the most money the guys at the top or the bottom? Who gets to go to lunch whenever they get hungry and gets to go play golf on Wednesday's? Verses those who make the least amount, have to go to lunch between twelve and one o'clock and gets fired on Thursday if they take off Wednesday to play golf.

In short, corporate America; what I call the traditional "A" plan, has failed many people over the years. This concept of working forty hours a week for forty years for no equity, building someone else's company and dream and if you are fortunate to make it to the end of the yellow brick road by avoiding involuntary separation from payroll; you get to be rewarded with retirement, living on half of what you could not make it on when you were being paid the full amount, is the chilling reality of most people who retire in this country. The simple fact is that most people who retire in this country retire below the poverty level. There is a better way for those of us who want more out of life. I call it a "B" plan.

The "B" plan or a "Better" plan is an option for you to consider that will give you the opportunity to build something for you and your family. The right "B" plan will give you your own income opportunity that will allow you to build equity for yourself while providing income streams that will give you the life that you want to live with the freedom of time that makes living a life worth living. There are some business owners who create businesses that turn out to be just another job they have created for themselves. What I am suggesting here is to find a company that is a business system that can operate with or without your presence by leveraging the efforts of others through building effective business relationships.

Robert Kiyosaki, in his best selling book, *Rich Dad, Poor Dad*, shares with his readers that a business system is a business that does not require your presence. He also shows a contrast between the thoughts and actions of his Rich Dad and his Poor Dad. Two very different people who have the ability to direct their financial futures as we all do. One dad (his poor dad) encouraged him to become an employee, while the other dad (his rich dad) encouraged him to become an entrepreneur. Robert learned that these two personalities have very different mind sets when it comes to business. Robert once said, "The world is filled with millions of small-business entrepreneurs who keep their leaky businesses afloat with hard work, sheer willpower, duct tape and baling wire. The problem is, if they stop working, the business breaks and sinks."

The millionaire mind set truly understands the power of leverage. One billionaire by the name of J. Paul Getty once stated, "I would rather have one percent of the efforts of one hundred people, than to have one hundred percent of my own efforts". We call this principle OPE, this stands for Other People's Efforts.

Another millionaire mind set is to use the principle of OPI, Other People's Ideas. A good example of this is Wendy's founder Dave Thomas. Dave realized from the success of other fast food outlets that by making small adjustments in the business model you can use what is working and just modify it slightly. Dave decided to make the burgers square and to call his fries "Biggie". Another example is the well known story of Bill Gates and Microsoft's MS DOS operating system. Bill Gates brought the rights to the operating system and used the idea to launch Microsoft. Someone else's idea, but Bill was able to see the big picture and leverage on its market potential. Another fact about this great entrepreneur Bill Gates, is that he offered to share ownership opportunities in Microsoft with several people with which he had a relationship. Three of them passed on the initial investment in Microsoft. But the others went on to invest, and as you know became billionaires. The three that passed on the deal remained poor because they did what so many people do everyday that don't have a millionaire mindset. Simply put they remain P.O.O.R. because they Pass Over Opportunities Repeatedly. How many ideas are out there that you come across everyday that you could leverage? Is the concept of relationship marketing one?

The next millionaire mindset is the principle of OPM; Other People's Money. Never let the excuse of not having the money stop you from pursuing your "B" plan and realize your dreams. Robert Kiyosaki referred to his poor dad as saying in times of lack, "we can't afford to do that"; however, his rich dad would make a different statement in the same situation by asking, "how can we afford it?". One mindset limited there options and shut down the creative process of the mind and the other mindset opens the mind to the possibilities of how to attract the resources needed to meet the need. There are many people who come to the shores of this great nation and start out with nothing and are able to use their mindsets to accumulate resources that allowed them to springboard into a "B" plan. Never let the lack of money stop you from implementing your "B" plan.

The final millionaire mindset that we want to highlight is the principle of OPO; Other People's Opinions. There are two sides to this coin. One perspective is to listen to those who have a track record of success in the area or endeavor that you have an interest in which you desire to be successful. One person said it like this; "to whom are you listening?"

Why would you listen to anyone about making money that has never made more money than what you have a desire to make? So many people listen to people who are not financially successful about a "B" plan about financial success that they know nothing about. It is natural for most people who have never been financially successful to any great extent to speak negatively about something they have no knowledge about. Avoid Other People's Opinions who fit this description.

The other side of the coin centers on your ability to make decisions quickly, when a "B" plan makes business sense and common sense. To the millionaire mind set that makes perfect sense. Napoleon Hill, in his classic book, *Think and Grow Rich*, stated that, "men who SUCCEED reach decisions PROMPTLY and change their minds, if at all, very slowly. Men, who FAIL, reach decisions IF AT ALL very SLOWLY and change their minds frequently and quickly". One must come to a place in their life where one can make a prompt decision about a "B" plan that they have heard or seen from someone who has the proven documented results, instead of asking someone their opinion about something they have not seen nor evaluated themselves. It is like going to a movie alone, but asking someone else who did not see the movie what they thought about the movie (whether it was good or bad). How can they give you their opinion about a movie that only you saw? Did they see the movie or Did you see the Movie?

Chapter 4:

The 3 Basic Rules of Success

Rule # 1: Stay Excited

In the mind of most, the term "stay excited" sounds like some cheap cheer at a pep rally or something that is really unnecessary or shallow. Yet, when this principle is understood in the fullness of the concept, you will be amazed and blown away about the importance and power of the first rule of success in relationship marketing. I was taught by many millionaire mentors that people will be more impressed by the Height of your Enthusiasm than the Depth of your Knowledge. No matter what your product or service may be, people that know you and even those that don't know you must be able to detect an above average passion flowing from you.

I remember when I first got out of the Military, people would always say to me that, "you need to loosen up some if you ever going to get someone to do business with you", and I would say and think that, "I have all the facts and knowledge and that would be all that I needed". Every time however, it seemed that just having "all the facts" with my Military personality would end up blowing up in my face in the world of relationship marketing. People never wanted to buy my facts and details stated in a boring manner. Instead, when I learned to get and "stay excited" with a smile on my face with the intensity of a robot and passion pouring out of my pores, people begin to join anything I was involved with or buy anything that I sold.

One day I was listening to a tape by Brian Tracey and I heard him say "people do business with people they like". He also pointed out that "we needed to like ourselves before we will send off impulses that show that we like others and are likable". Once I realized that people do business with whom they like and that the opposite is also true, I began to live by that simple principle. No matter how great the product or facts are; people don't do business with people they DON'T like. So, what I began to do was smile, laugh and try to have a sense of humor. Frankly put, just constantly staying excited around other people. I also would say to myself over and over again that, "I like myself, other people are going to like me as well and I will like them". In some situations, I would even tell the individual I'm doing business with "I like you". I discovered that people tend to want to be genuinely liked. Moreover, people gravitate towards people who have enthusiasm and positive energy. Let me ask you a question, who do you prefer to be around? Your positive friends or that friend that is always negative? So, ask yourself the question, which are you, the positive person that everyone prefers to be around or the negative person that you want to run from?

The rule stay excited moves into a deeper dimension when you think of stabilizing your emotions, not vacillating back and forth between being positive and negative. This can reflect an image of a person who has a lack of leadership and can show as a weakness to those around you. Some people around you are hoping for your success and others may be hoping for your failure. Yes, believe it or not we all have even family members that are not supportive and are hoping for our failure, so part of staying excited is to "Never let them see you Sweat".

Some years ago I learned a biblical principle that says, "a merry heart does good like medicine...", and once I realized the power of that principle, I began to incorporate humor into all my presentations in the relationship marketing game. People that miss this point don't understand the power of what "staying excited" will do with the added power of humor. Staying excited while using humor will also project positive energy whether you are the speaker or in an audience trying to assist the speaker who is presenting a sales presentation for you. Positive energy could be as simple as leaning forward in your chair, laughing at even the worst joke, not walking during a presentation, or simply looking at some with a radiant smile.

On the other hand, negative energy could be as simple as having folded arms and leaning back in the chair, allowing the cell phone to ring during a presentation, walking around distracting the audience and the presenter or simply having a conversation while a presenter is talking. A big part of the rule staying excited is to always say good things about everyone that is a part of your organization no matter what the person may have done or said destructive concerning you personally. If there is anything negative going on between you and someone else in your organization, address that issue with that individual or if that has already been exhausted, contact someone with experience or in a senior position to you that may already be seasoned with handling these types of issues and has a track record of stability and financial strength.

Be sure to avoid speaking negative about a team member because it can only hurt you in the long run. We always say "never put poison in your stream" you can never get all of it out of the stream and the poison begins to eat away at your organization. This can cause the destruction of a great team. Only send positive information downstream, so it can facilitate and promote growth throughout the team. Any issues that may be considered a negative most go "upstream" to someone who can help and only positive things go "downstream" to those with whom you may lead.

There may be times when you need to even encourage yourself in order to stay excited. Others can help you stay excited but it is better and more sustaining if you develop the capacity to encourage yourself to stay excited. In order to do this you have to be tuning in to the right channel in your mental attitude. Watching the right channel in your mind by focusing on being positive will make a difference in your excitement. Make sure you are not watching the Depression Channel, the This Won't Work Channel, the Complaining Channel, the Blaming Channel and everybody's favorite from time to time the I'm Tired Channel. Instead, turn your mind set to the Possibility Channel, the Victory Channel, the Lets make It Happen Channel and don't forget the Stay Excited Channel. The point is that you must tune in to the right channel on your "mind set" to stay excited. Learning to maintain the excitement and motivating others to stay excited will be a major part of your development as an effective leader in the relationship marketing industry.

Rule # 2 Stay Green and Growing

When I was 13 years old, I remember attending Shiloh Baptist Church in Selma Alabama. An old preacher decided to stop me one day and he made a statement to me that would forever change my life. He said, "Little Wilson always stay Green and Growing". I said "Uh"? He said, "Son, Stay Green and Growing" I said "What?" He said, "If you ever get to the point that you stop learning and think you know it all, you will have become ripe and you will fall off the tree and die, therefore, always stay green and growing". So, from that day forward I knew that if I was going to be successful, I must always be teachable and seek out new knowledge every day and to continue to improve on what I already knew.

I later heard a Millionaire say "You don't know what you don't know". Once again I was like "Uh...What?" He went on to say, "You know what you know and I know what I know, but you don't know what I know and I don't know what you know and you don't even know what you don't know". Wow, sometimes I get twisted up (and I don't know what I just said) when I try to explain this powerful principle. Simply put, there is always knowledge out there that is important to your success and you are not even aware that it exists or that it is important to your personal success. This concept is a state or mind that allows you to continue to absorb knowledge from people that are more successful in a given area than you. They may have gone before you and achieved greatness in various areas of their lives. Coming into this awareness that "you don't know what you don't know" is the beginning of staying green and growing; this will lead you to massive success.

I once heard someone share that 90% of the homes with a real estate value of at least 1 million dollars have a dedicated room as its library. Think about that, a room in the house dedicated to reading and studying. The rich understand the importance of learning new information. Stay green and growing fosters the principle that we must always be a student in life; a student of success. This is a learned behavior and is not developed by chance or accident. What a person in relationship marketing must do to master this step is to constantly listen to CD's, watch DVD's, read various books, attend trainings every time available (online, conference call or live), and be plugged into local weekly meetings and events (online, telephone or live) where you can network with other like minded people who become a vital source of information and support. You must be willing to trade ego for equity by Staying Green and Growing!

Rule # 3 Stay in the Game and Never Quit

This is probably the most important step of the 3 basic rules to success in relationship marketing. Why, because if you quit, throw in the towel and wimp out like a whiner instead of a winner you will never reach your full potential in any business. The majority of people don't stay constantly with one company long enough to see any true results. It is my personal opinion that most people will need at least four years to learn the art of really becoming successful with a given business, even if they have the right mentors and teachers. Others may take longer if they only want to do things their own way and not follow the advice of leaders who can help them.

One must make the commitment that, "I will not quit and I will learn everything I can in the process". One of the biggest problems is that some people quit before they can see the fruit of their labor. For example, I heard a story from a close friend about the Bamboo Tree. He stated that you have to plant the seed and water the blank hole in the ground everyday for two years without fail or the tree will never grow. Well, during the two years of watering that spot on the ground where the seed was planted and not seeing anything growing above the ground, it can be a little discouraging over time. Not to mention one might be viewed by everyone around like "you may be a little bit insane for watering a patch of dirt with no evidence that anything is growing there. Then, all of a sudden after two years of watering the bamboo tree, a small bud will sprout out of the ground and then, over the next 90 days they say the tree grows 80 to 90 feet tall. My friend said that this tree begins to grow so fast that a person can stand there and see it growing in front of their own eyes.

Now, my question for you is, "Did the tree grow in 90 days or did the tree grow over a two year and three month period?" It grew over the two year and three month period because for the first two years it was growing a massive root structure underground that could support the rapid growth of the tree above the ground over the three month period!

You see folks, in order to grow the bamboo tree from a seed, someone has to decide to water the tree "in faith" everyday, and not worrying about what they see above ground with the natural eyes over a two year period. It is the same way when growing a business. One must work at it everyday even if it appears that no progress is being made. They have to know that their efforts will yield fruit but their faith in the process must be sufficient to carry them through until the manifestation of the success that they are waiting to see. There is a principle I read in the Bible that says that a person must "walk by faith and not by sight". Another principle also states ... "Now faith is the substance of things hoped for and the evidence of things not seen". When people are unable to see any outward signs they must keep watering, keep working, keep staying in the game and never quit if they want to see success on a grand scale.

There are two major reasons to sticking it out and building your business for two to four years. The first reason is because during the process you will stumble across people that lead you to the networks of other people to help you build your business and you may meet them over the time period. Therefore, if you quit before that time you may not realize what you missed out on, and all of the people that you would have met and could have actually learned from.

The second reason for never ever quitting is the process of time that it takes to reprogram your thinking. This is important because most people have never been in business for themselves and the way that an employee thinks is different from how an entrepreneur thinks. The book, Think and Grow Rich by Napoleon Hill is a classic book highlighting the importance of how our thinking plays a role on our long term financial success. I read a story in the book which tells about this powerful principle to never quit. It is a true story about a miner who was digging for gold and he got discouraged and quit. The only problem was that he stopped "three feet from gold". The miner sold his land and gave up only selling it to someone else who dug three feet more to discover one of the largest gold finds ever.

I've asked tens of thousands of people all around the world this question; "Who out there will never, ever, ever quit?" And every time 99% of every audience will raise their hand in declare their allegiance to what company they are working for or building at that moment. My response is always the same when I see those hands go up, "We Will See"! We will see as soon as you receive some bad news or go through some tough time on the road to fulfilling your dreams. Or, let's say a person that you respect says something negative against your effort to achieve everything that was place in your heart while you are in the learning and watering stages of your business? Will you be able to hold on to your "Why" to keep you going regardless of other people's opinions or actions? They may attempt to steal your joy, your passion, your desire to stay in the game. When you can sit down and make sure you know your "Why", the reason you are striving for a particular goal, it can become the staying power you need. Your "Why" must become bigger than your "How". Then, you can truly "Stay" in the

Game and Never Ever Quit until you get to the End Zone, the Finish Line, the Home Plate or Beat the Buzzer as a Champion in Life.

Part Three: New Economy &

New School Class Begins

Chapter 5:
Yesterday's Keys Won't Fit in Today's Locks

Years ago I once heard someone say "Yesterday's keys won't fit in today's locks", when speaking about the need to change methods when the times have changed. Over the last two decades, we have seen a major change in our society. Some historians select fall of the Berlin Wall in 1989 as the end of the Industrial Age and the beginning of what we now call the Information Age. Our global economy has been clearly affected by this shift to the Information Age. Technology has made it a very small world indeed by increasing our ability to communicate and conduct business on a global scale with lightening speed unknown by those who only lived to see the Industrial Age. The Internet in particular has changed the way we do business.

Yet there many people still trying to hold on to some "old school" ways of doing business and it has greatly slowed their effectiveness in the marketplace. I once read, "If change does not take place from the top down voluntarily, it will take place from the bottom up through revolution". Now, I am not one who believes that all change is good; however, some change is necessary for progress. If leaders are not willing to change their methods of doing business in this new Information Age, they will find themselves losing valuable ground and may eventually find themselves left on the side lines. A good example of this from a business perspective was illustrated in the bestselling book *Good to Great: Why Some Companies make the Leap and Others Don't*, written by Jim Collins. He does a side by side comparison of two grocery chains; Kroger, a small value-based chain of supermarkets thriving in the 1950's and A&P the largest grocery chain in the world during that same time period. As technology increased during the sixties, both companies saw that the landscape was changing around them along with customer's preferences. Both companies conducted extensive market research, hired expert consultants to forecast future trends and built test stores.

The data they both collected was clear: the world was changing rapidly and customers were demanding convenience by desiring to do as much shopping as possible at one location. This is where it becomes interesting, because what these two companies DID with the same information made all the difference in their outcome. A&P ignored the data and stood on the side lines, while Kroger ACTED on it and developed the "superstore" strategy that we now see in the marketplace today. By 1999, Kroger had become the leading grocery chain in the country, generating profit eighty times that of its onetime competitor A&P. A&P found themselves waking up to a new day on the side lines of competitive business in their industry. Kroger positioned itself as a major player in the marketplace.

I remember reading a story about Albert Einstein when he was teaching as a professor. One of his student assistants was preparing a test for the next class session. The assistant asked, "Professor Einstein, which test are we going to give them?" To which Einstein responded, "The same test as last week." The assistant, now bewildered, asked, "But why give them the same test again?" To which Einstein said, "Because the answers are different this week."

In this Information Age, knowledge is increasing everyday and we can hardly keep pace with the change. Even just recently, we have changed the status of Pluto as a planet and are now using computers to map the entire DNA structure of human beings. Folks the challenges we face tend to not change as rapidly as the answers change for each of our challenges. Someone shared with me that the average college degree is outdated within five years of graduation. We must stay on top of learning and realize that a lifestyle of life long learning is necessary in order to stay current with our changing business climate in the Information Age.

Will Rogers was once quoted as saying, "You can be on the right track, but if you sit down you will eventually be run over". Even if we are "on the right track" in terms of business (i.e. a career, a business opportunity, or some other worthwhile pursuit); we must be sure to understand that changing times require us to develop new skill sets and to learn new ways of accomplishing our business objectives. Just recently, I became aware of an interesting statistic. Over 50% of the people who graduate from high school will never read an entire book to the end for the rest of their lives. Another interesting fact is that, the most read magazine in the homes across America is the TV Guide. Isn't it interesting that although most people who graduate from high school will not read an entire book from beginning to end for the rest of their lives, and that the most read magazine is the TV Guide, it speaks to why most people never live out their dreams because they spend little time developing themselves and more time watching other people live out their dreams or acting out a fantasy not their own on TV. There are many sitting on "the track" that just might lead to fulfilling a life that others could only dream about if they would only get up and BE the person they were created to become. Some people never leave the shores of contentment because they are too afraid to discover new oceans of life. Yesterday's keys won't fit in today's locks.

Chapter 6
Using Technology to
Leverage Your Efforts

Telephone Techniques

Cold calling is used in the industry of relationship marketing on a regular basis. The problem with it is that it is not a very efficient use of our time. It is only a one time event and can waste a lot of time if you don't get a sale or make an appointment. We have found that it is better to get a prospect to call you rather than you cold calling them. Furthermore, cold calling is risky in that you have to be mindful of not calling those who are on the National Do Not Call list. Most people who receive cold calls are not very warm and fuzzy when a stranger is calling them to sell something. So how do you create a situation where the caller is calling you instead of you having to call them? This is one question that we hope to share an answer with you by the time your finish reading this book, because it is at the heart of maintaining an ongoing cycle of new leads who are hunting you down for what you have to offer.

Selling and prospecting are not the same. One is prospecting when a qualified lead is calling you rather than you cold calling to those with whom you then have to sell. There are several ways to generate leads that are tracking you down rather than you calling people who are considered cold call contacts. We will cover some of those lead generation techniques later in this chapter and how to put it all together in a marketing system that you can put on autopilot in the chapter on "The Marketing System". For now, let us focus on what to do when the call comes in to you from a prospect who is responding to your marketing efforts.

It is important from the start to project an image of professionalism. This establishes the initial impression of your prospect about your organization. How your phone is answered and the tone in which you handle your prospect will set the direction of the rest of the call. Or if you are making an out bound call to someone with whom you are responding, the way you speak to them will go a long way if you are professional, warm and clear in your communication. I often use a third party to receive calls and to return calls in order to give the level of professionalism that I expect when conducting business. An outside (contract) live answering service, contract telemarketer, appointment setter or executive assistant (virtual or contract) will work just fine. Many of these services are inexpensive and can be contracted on a month to month basis as needed. We have found that the most effective way of using the telephone is to not make the call or answer it yourself. This allows you to only spend time talking with those prospects who want to talk with you instead of wasting time talking to those who are not interested. If someone takes time to call or respond to a marketing piece you developed, then they have shown some interest in talking with you. Be sure to make the best initial impression that you can.

There are several 800 number services available to use for pennies a day, in order to receive calls from prospects that you then can forward to one of the services mentioned above to answer for you. Seeing a toll free number in order to respond to a marketing piece gives prospects more of a comfortable feeling that they are dealing with a legitimate company. As long as you maintain a professional confident tone over the phone, prospects will give tremendous respect to you and your organization, which ultimately creates a sense of power and organization that people tend to like when conducting business. Using the professional services of third party services like a professional answering service or contract executive assistant will result in a lot more appointments than if you handle the calls because these people are professionals and skilled in what they do on your behalf. Once they have qualified each of your leads, then you can speak to them with the objective of closing a qualified prospect. It is very impressive to have an executive assistant (virtual or otherwise) to follow up on your leads and will give you much more of an advantage when talking to your prospects by phone appointment or in person.

Voice Messaging Broadcasting Systems

There is technology available that will automatically send out bound calls to prospects that record your voice message or the recording of a professional.

Whatever message you choose it can greatly reduce the time it takes to get your message out to many people in a short period of time. This prospecting tool is efficient and effective, while also very cost effective. Using this technology in conjunction with a lead generation system that initially collected their contact information is one way to follow up with interested prospects. Information on your follow up call can be information as simple as communicating dates and times of conference calls or instructions on registering for an upcoming event. With the use of this kind of technology, you can literally contact thousands of prospects within minutes who will call you back within minutes of sending an effective voice communication. This gives you a serious edge when marketing your products or services. It's like having hundreds of telemarketers calling and qualifying prospects for you at a very cost effective rate. There are even techniques that you can use to get paid to prospect by using this tool that we will go over in more detail in the chapter entitled The Marketing System.

E-Mail and Auto responders

Years ago there were limited ways to make initial contact with a potential customer. They include various forms of advertising, direct mail, door to door and by telephone contact. Now with the Internet we have the ability to communicate with thousands of people within a few seconds for a fraction of the cost of traditional methods. This tool allows for overcoming many of the barriers that may have traditionally prevented the person you wanted to contact from even receiving your message. For example, trying to reach a prospect by phone presents challenges like, getting past a gatekeeper (i.e. secretary, receptionist, etc.) who will be sure to screen calls and quickly divert marketing calls to the voice mail box that no one checks. Also, if you happen to reach the person you are calling, they could be busy and unable to talk or simply distracted by other day to day issues.

With the use of e-mail you can send a detailed accurate message directly from you (the sender) and be sure that when it is opened by the recipient they will read exactly what you intended to communicate without the translation of someone who may have taken an inaccurate phone message. Most people will respond to a well communicated e-mail that was sent as a result of requesting information from you. We will show you how to get prospects to opt in or request an email communication from you in the chapter on the Marketing System.

There are many reasons that people will respond to your e-mail rather than returning your telephone call. Some of them include the fact that they know what the e-mail is in reference to and why it was sent. They can also review it when they have the time at their convenience and it only takes a few seconds to read and respond. This way of communicating is becoming a global standard.

If you really want to maximize your e-mail communication power, you can use an auto responder system. An auto responder is an archive of prewritten e-mails that you can manually send to a list of prospects or they can be automatically sent for you as you desire. E-mail systems are now so easy to use and can provide many different ways to deliver e-mails to a few people up to thousands of people for a very low cost. There are many online services available and they usually cost a flat rate per month (around $20.00 on average). This system can send e-mails to predetermined contacts or prospects at various intervals and can save significant time over having to do the same manually. After the initial set up, all you have to do is write your e-mails and set the time intervals and to whom you would like them to be sent. Add additional names as you gather other contacts or prospects and the rest is done for you by the system. You can set up different series in most auto responder accounts. You can also send out a periodic newsletter to a list of contacts based on a schedule you choose (i.e. weekly, monthly, etc.).

Video e-mails can be sent to various contacts and statistics reveal that the response rates on these types of e-mails are 30 times greater than with regular e-mail. People love the ability to see the person talking to them on video. With this option, you simply record your video message until you have it exactly like you want, then enter your e-mail addresses and click send. Once you get the hang of it, using e-mail communication to boost your efficiency and increase your sales becomes far more effective than worn out and time consuming traditional methods of old.

Web Site Presence

If you have a company or are selling products for a company, it is a strong probability that it has a web site. If not, get one quickly. Moreover, you need a personal web site that can highlight your personal, professional expertise and what you have to offer to the world. That's right; I said a personal web site. The Internet is one of the most powerful forms of leverage that you can have. While you are sleep, this site can inform potential prospects of who you are and what you have of value that anyone in the world can access. Remember from the previous chapters, we shared the importance of presenting yourself as an expert and showing value so that others will want to follow you as a leader in your particular industry or niche. A personal and professional web site set up specifically about you, helps to establish your value in the minds of prospects. This site will act as an electronic net that will bring in leads for you by communicating what you have to offer.

Build your web site with a clear, concise theme that is based around a niche and that is supported by an abundance of quality articles and helpful information on your topic. Choosing a theme can be the hardest part because it requires a little research unless you know a lot about a hobby or subject area.

Once it is set up, you must include this web address on all of your correspondence (letterhead, business cards) and other marketing materials. Remember, it is important to establish value in the eyes of each of your prospects, so the purpose of this site is not to advertise your product or service, this can be done on your company site. The purpose of this site is to market your expertise, your personal value to the prospect. You may provide a place where prospects can receive a free e-newsletter from you or a free article from you on a subject of interest. In order to send it to them, you must provide a place to capture their name and email address. Building an opt in email list is one of the best ways to gather prospects. Offer a newsletter or an e zine. Building relationships with affiliates will also lead you to some really interesting experiences and meeting some good contacts and prospects. Be sure to only send the article or e-newsletter after you have collected this contact information. You will find that the contact information is your most valuable asset and will produce ongoing contact and marketing opportunities with those who consider you a valuable resource. This is very powerful.

Setting up a web site is so easy these days that you can do it yourself. For those of you who are intimidated by the thought of that; you can go to many web based companies sites that build and host web sites. This is a valuable resource for those who don't know how to build a web site or those who simply don't want to take time to do so. There are countless people who are using the web to make millions all over the world and many of them have no formal education or computer expertise. If you want to know how to do something, it is someone in cyberspace that can show you inexpensively and sometimes for free. Getting your personal web site is a key to creating value in the eyes of your prospects and producing leads that will fuel your main business product or service. We also have additional resources at our companion web site to this book at: www.howtowininrelationshipmarketing.com.

Weblogs

A weblog is basically a public online diary that allows publishers (bloggers) to create and post information in a reverse chronological order. Most people use it as such (entertainment, voice concerns or to just be sociable); however, by using it for business purposes you can maximize the marketability of your value as well as the service or product you have to offer. You can pick up qualified prospects within 48 to 72 hours through the skillful use of weblogs. Your objective is to provide informative content while attracting qualified prospects that will eventually purchase what you have to offer. There is a delicate balance in writing content for your blog to insure that you don't sound like you are advertising something. Visitors will get the impression that you are trying to sell them something and the blog will not accomplish its overall purpose.

The blog should be used to share information or express your thoughts about a particular area that visitors have an interest. You can place throughout the content of your blog links to your service or product sites that visitors will eventually click on once you have established your value to them. Don't include your blog address on your initial contact with prospects. You may want to do so at a later time with e-mails that you send out via auto responder by noting at the bottom of a communication a brief "Visit my blog" message.

Weblogs rank high with search engines, which mean that when people are searching for information on the topic(s) you discuss on your blog, there is a high probability that your address will rank high in the listings. Weblogs typically are content rich because they are "keyword rich". In short, weblogs tend to be one long page of content with lots of text and multiple entries, unlike web sites that have multiple pages with limited text on each page. Therefore, when you set up your weblog, be sure to set the number of entries high so that you can position your weblog to receive high ranking among the search engines.

Here are some important facts about weblogs to keep in mind:

- Blogs can be an inexpensive way to generate free traffic from search engines, other blogs and social marketing web sites.

- Blogs are easy to set up and maintain while providing an online presence and creating content.

- You can use them as an enhancement to other online marketing efforts like articles, press releases, video emails and other marketing tools.

- Blogs are interactive in nature because people can leave comments. They tend to be more credible than other types of online marketing efforts as long as you are providing real value for your visitors.

When choosing a weblog platform, be sure to note that there are two basic platforms to choose from. The first is called stand alone or open source blogging. There are many developers who contribute to the associated software by constantly adding components and extensions called "plugins" to improve the functionality of the particular software. This platform allows for the greatest flexibility and control over the weblog site. There are several free sites that offer this platform and you can go to our web site at www.howtowininrelationshipmarketing.com to check out the most up to date listing of resources available. They change on a regular basis so we choose to keep them on our site for the most accurate resources available to our readers.

The second weblog platform is called a hosted blog platform. There are various services that offer an easy to set up hosted blog that will get a sub-domain name for your blog. The hosted sites are easy to set-up and several are free (see our site for listing) but they tend to have less flexibility and control over the site.

Both platforms have there limitations and advantages, but most entrepreneurs and business owners use the stand alone platform over the hosted platform. For more detailed information on how to set up your blog and how to launch it; you can go to our web site at www.howtowininrelationshipmarketing.com and click on resources for more information.

There are many tools mentioned in this chapter that can help you leverage your marketing efforts. Some of these methods have costs associated with them. In the next chapter we will show you how to fund your advertising efforts and offset some of the costs associated with the methods mentioned in this chapter. In essence, show you a powerful strategy that, if used correctly, will position you to get paid to advertise even when your prospect doesn't purchase your main service or product offering.

Chapter 7:
Funded Proposals "Getting Paid to Advertise Your Business"

This concept is very powerful and if used correctly, it can have a tremendous impact on your current business. A funded proposal is the strategy of selling an inexpensive, yet useful information product or service to cover your advertising expenses, and then providing your main product or service on the back end once an initial relationship is established with a prospect. It allows you to generate qualified leads that purchase the inexpensive funded proposal, while turning that new prospect into a customer. Now that you have established a customer relationship, it is now easier to sell an upgraded product or service (your main product or service) to an existing customer rather than to a total stranger who has no relationship to you. The money that you generate from the funded proposal should cover the cost of advertising at minimum but can also be a source of small profit to pay for continued advertising efforts. In short, you are getting paid to advertise.

Let's use some examples that may provide some practical understanding. A real estate agent obviously wants to sell houses; which is their main service offering. A real estate agent can do the normal advertising like other real estate agents or they can use a funded proposal to gather leads that will eventually turn into contracts on houses for sale or clients looking to purchase houses. We will recommend to our real estate agent to create a booklet or online course seminar on "How to Get the Maximum Price for Your Home in Any Market". In her marketing efforts the agent might give a description of the course as follows: Get on average an extra 15% to 20% more value than other homes in your area by learning the secretes to maximizing your home's price. This course will make you thousands more the next time you put your home on the market while cutting the time listed by over half.

This course might be available online as an e-book or provided through the mail in booklet form for $29.95. This becomes the agent's funded proposal offer. The agent advertises this offer then collects information from prospects who are interested in the topic. Now the agent has sold information and the sale of this information has reduced the cost of advertising for the funded proposal. Moreover, let's think about what else has just happened. The agent now has someone who may be in the market to sell a home sometime in the future and can now establish a relationship and regular contact with someone who may list a home with them. The contact information (the name and e-mail or address and phone number) becomes a very valuable asset. Now the agent has gained a customer (from the funded proposal) and can now place the contact information into an e-newsletter, provide information on their weblog, and can plug information into the voice message broadcast on specials or other offers.

Now, when the customer is ready to sell a home, guess who comes to mind? Our real estate agent. I know that someone reading this may be saying, "but what if they don't call the real estate agent and list their property with them?". Good question, the answer is simple, the prospect that did not list a home with our agent has at least helped to cover advertising expenses that may have closed another prospect who did decide to purchase or list a home with our agent.

Let's use another example. What if we had a person who was selling a health care product that cured a particular illness? That person could develop a funded proposal that is an inexpensive "how to" product that provides a health benefit or solution to their pain or discomfort for $19.95. Using the same steps mentioned earlier, even if they did not buy the main product, the person advertising this product could still earn income to offset advertising costs. At best, the prospect will find value in the funded proposal and eventually buy the main product. This is basic direct sales, which provides an automatic lead, an automatic sale and fast cash flow to pay for the costs of advertising or even become a profitable offering. In the later chapters we will show you how to put it all together in a system that can be a powerful tool to build your company's revenues while reducing or eliminating advertising costs.

It is important to note as we close this chapter, that the funded proposal is used in conjunction with our traditional advertising medium such as but not limited to; print media of newspapers, magazines, and flyers along with their electronic versions (i.e. e-zines etc.). Radio and TV advertising can be done also once the marketing system we will further discuss in the later chapter of the same title is mastered. The funded proposal will be the world's first introduction to you and the value that you can offer, while all the while creating leads that will be eventually exposed to your main or higher end product service or business opportunity later on in your marketing system cycle.

Part Four:

Leadership Development

"You Incorporated"

Chapter 8:
People Don't Just Join Teams; They Join Effective Leaders

As discussed in previous chapters, your overall success in marketing your main product, service or business opportunity will come down to how well people connect with and see you as a leader. The value that you as a person can bring to the table is ultimately your foundation for any business relationship that you will develop as a business leader. If it is a matter of marketing a product or service you have to offer or simply trying to recruit an employee or business associate that will bring a certain skill set you need to your team or organization; your perceived value in the mind of that prospect or team member will have a critical role in whether they are influenced to join your team or purchase what you have to offer. It is all a function of leadership.

Leadership has been defined as the ability to influence. Everyone has someone that they play a role in influencing every day. How well one is able to influence people in various situations speaks to the level of leadership that they have with that particular group. For example, in a family, someone plays a role in influencing various family members in some situation during a typical day. Mom might have a leadership role in determining what the family will eat

71

for the day, while Dad might play a leadership role of influence in a particular situation about whether a child of driving age can use the family car for the evening. A child might even play a leadership role in a particular situation about when they are ready to eat. Especially, when they are a few months old and they are screaming and crying at the top of their lungs (which is their way of communicating a need at that age). As a parent, you are being influenced or led by that child's actions at that moment to do something. Likewise, in other environments like among friends, businesses, religious organizations and educational environments, just to name a few type of groups that we interact with daily, we are constantly consciously or unconsciously being influenced (led) or influencing (leading) someone in a group (formal or informal) of people. My examples here are only to illustrate the simple principle that, everyone in every group or organization has the ability to influence the activities of others within that group. Where there are at least two people involved in some activity, someone is leading and someone is following at some point during the activity. Roles of influence may change at any given point, but there is a constant lead and follow exchange of influence during the activity. Leadership is influence.

The level of the effectiveness of our leadership depends on how skilled we are at accomplishing some activity that requires the cooperation of two or more people. I once heard it put like this, "if you think you are leading, just look around you; if no one is following then all you have done is gone on a nice walk". When leadership is exercised in a manner that influences others to accomplish a task, goal or activity, then leadership is considered effective. As previously mentioned, all of us have the "ability" to influence or lead others; but effective leadership gets something done. We often say "only results count," and in business only the results that translate into revenue generation count. Obviously we are all in business to make money and the end result is making a profit. Profit is the amount of money left over after the transaction is completed. Leadership in business is measured by many standards; however, profit is a very important measurement of how effective a leader is in business. We all know that companies will not produce a profit at all times, particularly during start up phases and certain time cycles of business. However, if you are in business for any extended period of time and you are not producing a profit at some point of the life of the business, you may not have a business you just may have a hobby or charitable organization. In my mind there are two important rules in business. The first rule is: I must have fun doing the business. The second rule is: making money is more important than having fun. You see if I am just having fun and not making money, I am just having fun. In order for it to be a business enterprise, I must make money.

For example, a sky diver has to enjoy (have fun) jumping out of airplanes; however, if the sky diver does not learn the fundamental skill sets it takes to safely land on every jump, then their jumping career is over! So, jumping out of the airplane is rule number 1 (having fun); but landing safely is the most important goal (safety) because without that the sky diver can't jump another day. In business, having fun is the motivation to get up everyday to do the business, the thing that keeps you going during challenging times. In short, fun is the passion that fuels your activity. Profit or making money is the fuel that insures that you can keep the business open. Without either of those elements one will be hard pressed to keep a business going for the long term. Now, what does this have to do with leadership?, you may be asking. And the answer is that effective leadership has everything to do with a successful enterprise. Our ability to effectively lead or influence people must be developed and improved over time. This takes effort on our part to gain knowledge and to develop skills to increase our effectiveness as leaders. Although we all will lead in life, how effective we are as leaders is determined by what we learn about effective leadership. We are all born to be leaders, but we are not born with leadership skills. How effective we are in our leadership is a function of the skills we learn and how we use those skills we have learned to lead or influence people to accomplish great things.

At the heart of leadership is service. Serving others must be the motivation that drives our desire to lead. There is a principle that I use as the foundation of my leadership philosophy and it stands as the "why" behind all that I do as a leader; "great leadership must be born out of great service to others". One must be willing to sincerely want to serve those that they lead or have a desire to influence. Without this foundation, leadership is cold and will not have a lasting effect on those being led. Loyalty cannot be developed in those who follow a leader if they sense that the leader does not care about them. Someone put it this way, "people don't care how much you know until they know how much you care". How much you care comes out in your ability to serve the people you influence. The greatest leaders of all time who positively affected the course of human events had this understanding.

From a business perspective, serving your people should be the glue that holds your team or organization together. People are attracted to those who bring value of expertise to the table. This is step one in the marketing process. The next step in the process is determined by how well you serve them with that expertise. This will determine if the prospect is willing to following you for the long term. The initial attraction is sparked in the eyes of the prospect by what you know (your expertise in solving a problem or meeting a need), loyalty is created in how well you serve them with that knowledge or expertise. So the combination of knowledge and service create the long term value of your leadership to those who follow. The leaders with the most powerful relationships with people can pick up a phone or send out an email and move large amounts of people to act as one to accomplish a specific task. It is this type of leadership that is at the heart of successful relationship marketing.

A key characteristic of effective leadership is your ability and willingness to lead yourself through adversity and challenge. No one will want to follow you if you do not have the ability to lead yourself and others through struggles. Those that you lead gain tremendous respect and confidence in a leader who has been proven through difficult circumstances. You want to be a leader in all aspects of your life but especially when it comes to your business.

Another characteristic of leader that attracts those who desire to follow or be influenced by your leadership is the leader's ability to stay focused on accomplishing the goal while facing outside criticism. Leaders will always have someone to criticize them and their decisions. You will not always make the right decisions but whatever the decision you make in any given situation, you will have those who stand on the sidelines and criticize your actions. Don't let that affect your focus. Stay the course.

Effective leaders tend to have a lot of rules that they personally or professionally follow and expect those who follow to live up to the same to accomplish the corporate goal. They tend to treat themselves with integrity and they tend not to tolerate disrespect from others for any extended period of time. This is handled by ignoring the offending party or removing them from interaction.

Effective leaders tend to have a possibility mindset or an abundance mentality. This mentality keeps effective leaders from the fear of loss.

Chapter 9:
Invest In Your Professional Leadership Development

In the previous chapter we discussed what leadership is and its role in building your successful business or marketing efforts. In this chapter we will focus on the process of leadership development. The most important thing one must realize about leadership development is that it is a process not a destination. It is also as personal and individual as you are as a person, based on where you are in your leadership journey. Developing our leadership does not end with the reading of a particular book, the completion of a certain class or seminar or the viewing of a particular video or DVD. All of these can contribute to the development of our leadership skills; but no one magic pill exists that one can take to become the ultimate leader. It is not a sprint but rather a marathon of learning how to use certain tools and information available to us and walking out our new found knowledge among those with whom we have influence. Our desire should be to get better at it everyday.

Resources abound with information and training on leadership. My suggestion is to get your hands on every book or course you can that will help to develop your leadership skills and other skill sets that will positively contribute to build you, your team and ultimately your business. We have a list of some resources that are available for your leadership development at www.howtowininrelationshipmarketing.com. This list is in no way a complete list of resources available, but should give you start on your leadership development journey.

I once read that who you are becoming over the next five years can be easily determined now by some very important indicators. In the next five years, we will become more like the people we spend the most time with (i.e. friends, family coworkers, mentors), the books that we choose to read, the words we choose to listen to (i.e. music, radio) and the things we choose to observe (TV shows, types of movies). The sum total of who we will become is currently tied to our habits in these areas that we have now. If you like what you are doing in these areas now and it is taking you in the direction of the type of progress you want to make in business or in your financial future, then well done. However; if you are not pleased with one or more of these areas, the good news is that you can change it. This is a big planet with over 6 billion people and many places all over the world in which to live and lots of information at your finger tips through the Internet that you can invest your time to develop your leadership skills. Formal and informal educational opportunities are present from anywhere on the globe. You can truly become the leader you were created to become by developing a plan and consistently working on that plan daily, little by little until you find yourself being the leader you were meant to be. Whatever the perceived limitations you may think exist in your mind; they are just that; limitations that exist in your own mind. We hope that this book in some way will help move you to action in becoming all that you can be while pointing you in the right direction to resources that can help you in your leadership journey.

Today is the first day of the rest of your life, and you truly have the steering wheel of your destiny in your hands. It doesn't matter where one starts, it matters where one ends up when you take your last breath. The journey is the most important thing in our leadership development. Change takes place from the inside out. You have the power to change your world by creating the world in you that you want to live in around you. A good example of that is a story I once read about a gentleman who had invented dynamite explosives. His name was Alfred Nobel. He was reading one day an obituary of his deceased brother and as he read it he realized that the newspaper had made a mistake in its description of his brother. In fact they had made an error and had written the obituary about his life and not about his deceased brother. The obituary explained how his invention had resulted in the destruction of many lives during the war. After reading the potential legacy he would leave to society, he chose to change that legacy by contributing something to peace rather than war. Mr. Nobel founded an organization with the aim of awarding people for peace. His award, the "Nobel Peace Prize" has awarded many for their contribution to promoting peace around the world. This is but one example of many that shows that it doesn't matter where you start, what matters is the way you finish.

As additional proof to this principle I have assembled below a small sample of people who may have had a rough time starting out but over time developed as leaders in their chosen areas of influence.

Shawn "Puffy" Combs was placed in special education as a child but went on to create a music empire generating revenues in excess of $300 million dollars annually.

Henry Ford went bankrupt 5 times before he successfully built the Ford Motor Company.

Thomas Edison tried over 10,000 failed attempts at creating the light bulb until he finally accomplished his goal. He was once quoted as saying that he ran out of things that would not work until he finally stumbled upon what would work. His laboratory burnt to the ground before this great discovery, but that did not stop him from accomplishing his goal.

Did you know that Albert Einstein did not speak until the age of 4 and did not read until the age of 9? Yet, he went on to become a major contributor to Science.

A businessman by the name of Mr. Macy was arrested for tax evasion and overcame this obstacle. He went on to start a successful department store chain that we now know as the brand Macy's.

Anita Baker sent her demo tape to every record company in the country, only to have Arista Records send her a letter basically telling her "not to quit her day job". She went on to become one of the major Diva's in American Pop music.

Can you believe that, Luther Vandross was booed off stage on three separate occasions at the Apollo Theater? His long successful career as a leader in the music industry and as a vocalist is unmatched in class and quality.

Don King was convicted of manslaughter and served time in prison. After his release he was able to begin a successful career as a promoter, a profession for which he had no previous experience. His company generates hundreds of millions of dollars every year.

John Bunyan wrote the *"Pilgrim's Progress"*, which is among one of the finest of English literature. This he accomplished after he had been confined in prison, sorely and unjustly punished, because of his views on the subject of religion.

Tim Allen "The Tool Man" went on to be very successful in the long running sitcom television show *"Home Improvement"* after he had served time in prison on drug charges. He is also successful on the big screen in movies.

Charles Dutton "Rock" served time in prison for murder and went on to a long career in television and movies.

Even the authors of this book, have had their share of challenges and disappointments that could have had a negative impact on our leadership development. We are sure that if we sit down and talk to each of you reading this book that you can share some sad stories and challenging experiences that could be used to give an excuse for not stepping up to the challenge of becoming the leader you were created to be. We all have the potential for great leadership inside of us and the power to make a choice to develop the skills to cultivate that greatness regardless of past mistakes or wherever we may have started.

The excuses of your past or your current circumstances; they should never play a role in stopping you from becoming the leader that you were created to be. Like so many who have gone before you, you can acquire the knowledge and tools you need to become the leader you have been created to become. You make the difference. Invest in your leadership development.

Part Five:

Business Development

"Building an Effective

Marketing System"

Chapter 10:
The Marketing System

This is the chapter where we put it all together. What you will learn in this section is a combination of the author's over 60 years of combined experiences in business and relationship marketing. All of our experiences along with what we have learned over the years from others cannot possibly be covered in one section of a book or for that matter within one book. Nevertheless, we have provided for you in this section as much as practical, because we realize that those who read this material will come from various experiences and levels of business knowledge. This section will outline the tools and methods we have used that have made us together as well as individually a success over the years in business. We will also take some of the information we shared in previous chapters and show you how to map out a system that will help you maximize your marketing efforts and leverage your time as well.

We mentioned in previous chapters the importance of using technology to help you manage and track your business activities. As you develop the systems that best fit your style of doing business, you will discover what works best for you. Our world is constantly changing and no one has "the only right answer" to the system that will be your perfect formula. We hope that you can take some of our best practices and use them to help build the system that is right for you.

So how do you get the phone to ring with prospects that are chasing you down to get more information about what you have to offer? Let's get to the answer.

Getting People to Chase You Down

There are many techniques that we have used that drive the initial contact process. Remember the chapter on the funded proposal? This is the foundation for building a steady flow of callers who are interested in how to build their business. I once read that 95% of the people you talk to will never become a part of your business opportunity when you first meet them and only try to offer them your opportunity. I am not sure how accurate that number is but it is close based on the years of experience I have had in marketing and sales. People don't like being sold to; however, they don't mind acquiring knowledge on how to do something that will help them improve their success. The key here is to advertise your retail product, your how to... funded proposal on the front end, while keeping in contact with your new customer to eventually share your business opportunity.

It is much easier to turn a retail customer into an interested business associate with your company because the relationship is already in place. Many huge money earners are initially marketing and promoting inexpensive information products not directly related to their main business offering; rather they become experts in meeting the needs of prospects. The most important activity that you have is building a large amount of contacts with other relationship marketers and maintaining relationships with them. This activity will fund your marketing efforts now while building your business in the long term.

Your first source of lead generation is someone who is looking for your company or products specific to your company. These are the most effective leads because they are looking for your company or the products or services your company provides. They have an emotional interest to buy but are trying to logically justify the purchase. In order to get these people to contact you, use the personal web site we talked about in a previous chapter. Advertise yourself, your team and your marketing system. The replicated site your company provided will not work. There are too many of them with the same content to point people to you!

Next, you must create ads that drive traffic to your web site. Stay away from pay per click for now. Unless you are a Google Adwords expert, these ads could cost you $10 to $30 each and that could be cost prohibitive. Generate Free traffic by using the world's largest website where you can place classified ads to generate interest in you, your team and your business. These ads, if written effectively can drive lots of traffic to your website. There are many other free classified ad sources, but we mention this one because it is the most popular: www.CraigsList.org .

The next step is to create a capture page for prospects to go to in order to find out more information on you or your business. This capture page should provide a place for the visitor to put their name and email address. Please note that you should be making an offer here as you initially described in your ad placed, for a free report or your funded proposal. Only something of value will interest the visitor to leave their contact information.

Another way to generate traffic is by posting an online video of you giving out critical information of value to those who are interested. Again your funded proposal can be the lead in that drives people who are clicking on your ad to leave contact information or purchase your funded proposal. Be sure to define your target market before you start recording your video. Create a clear purpose then call them to action. Also be sure to tell prospects to go to your web site or capture page for more information.

The next step in your marketing system is to drive traffic to your web site by creating press releases. The first major way to get traffic from press releases is through the search engines. By writing the press release with key words, you can have an impact on how it will be listed on the search engines. The second way is to get a submission service. These services will give you space on their site and promote it while giving you huge exposure. A press release is simply an announcement or an explanation of a service or product.

Use your blog to drive traffic to your site. This is a very important piece to your overall marketing strategy. Be sure to have good content and use links conservatively to direct people to your web site. Be sure to educate your visitors and they will continue to come back. Update your blog regularly.

You can choose to provide a telephone number for those who feel compelled to call. Be sure to use a live answering service to take your call and answer in your company name. You can get these services for as low as $40 per month and a small per call fee. This will position you in the mind of a prospect that you are a professional. The answering service should have an email address for you so that you can follow-up with the caller. You may return the call or simply direct them to your web site capture page to purchase your inexpensive funded proposal or obtain your free information report. If they purchase your funded proposal, now you have just made money on driving free traffic to your web site. This is very powerful and can be done automated or manually.

Please note that in this Information Age, prospects have less of a need to speak with a sales person. And this need is reducing even more everyday. Why do they need to speak to a sales person, when the information they need can be provided online? In the old days, it was important to be in the right place at the right time. In the Information Age, you can be in all places at all times. Your message must reach potential prospects in multiple ways and at a variety of times. By leveraging time saving systems you duplicate your own efforts through the use of technology and a well planned marketing system. Our purpose is to gain the prospects interest without cold calling and to receive their permission to receive further communication from you.

For more detailed information on developing a marketing system or to gain resources on using marketing systems already developed for you, please visit us at www.howtowininrelationshipmarketing.com.

Chapter 11:

A Call to Action "Don't Just Speak About

It, Be About It!"

Often times, we can read a book like this and say at the end, "that was good information". You could also say, "one day I'll do some more research to see if this will work for me". I once heard from someone that, "Procrastination is the Graveyard to Opportunity". So many people go through life just speaking about what they need to do rather than being about what they should become. Our hope is that you allow the information in this book to become a part of you. Moreover, in some way we would have contributed to your "being".

In his book, Zen in the Martial Arts, Joe Hyams defines the term dojo:

"A dojo is a miniature cosmos where we make contact with ourselves - our fears, anxieties, reactions, and habits. It is an arena of confined   conflict where we confront an opponent who is not an opponent but rather a partner engaged in helping us understand ourselves more fully. It is a place where we can learn a great deal in a short time about who we are and how we react in the world. The conflicts that take place inside the dojo help us handle conflicts that take place outside. The total concentration and discipline required to study martial arts carries over to daily life. The activity in the dojo call on us to constantly attempt new things, so it is also a source of learning-in Zen terminology, a source of self enlightenment."

We hope in some way that this book can be a source of enlightenment for you on your business journey. Your journey in business will be much like the dojo. You will face many opponents to your success and learn many lessons. As you follow your dreams to success and financial freedom, know that we are willing to provide you with some of the resources that will help you accomplish your desires. Business is a part of life's journey and we hope you always remember, "Everyday is Thanksgiving, every meal is a feast and every minute is a lifetime; we have a lifetime to enjoy life, so Enjoy the Journey!

Reader Only Content Bonus Materials

There was so much more we wanted to include in this book, but space did not permit us to reveal this valuable information here. We have placed hidden passwords through out this book to allow you access to exclusive bonus material we have included on our companion web site at:

www.howtowininrelationshipmarketing.com

Be sure to visit the web site for more information on how you can win in relationship marketing.

About the Authors

T.V. Wilson

T.V. Wilson was nominated by his State House of Representatives Member to attend the U.S. Air Force Academy. Upon graduation, he served in the military during the Desert Storm Conflict. As an entrepreneur, he founded and had success as the owner of a restaurant, a child development center and several other ventures. He also founded a school for academic excellence and later became the Executive Producer and host of his own television series that aired on a Fox affiliate.

He has been a successful relationship marketer for over 20 years and is recognized as one of the top earners in the company he represents. He has been awarded with his company's diamond ring which represents that he earned a seven figure income within a twelve month period. He has spoken to and trained thousands of entrepreneurs in the industry of relationship marketing and loves to reveal the secrets to his success on how he earns seven figures a year in this industry.

Steve Branch

Steve Branch considers himself a "sports and entertainment enthusiast", and his track record of starting numerous successful companies in that industry has proven those words to be an accurate description of this entrepreneur. With over 20 years of owning and operating a chain of restaurants, clubs and lounges along with his launching and operating other related companies such as an artist management company, a record label and a concert promotions company; he would readily admit that relationship marketing is his favorite type of business.

He has had 20 years experience as a relationship marketing entrepreneur and has earned in one year over 1 million dollars from the industry. He wears a ring from his company signifying that he earned over seven figures within twelve months and continues to have phenomenal success in the industry. He speaks to thousands of entrepreneurs around the world every year and enjoys sharing information on how others can become financially free.

Thomas Hofler

Thomas Hofler is a leadership and organizational development coach who has trained hundreds of entrepreneurs on how to plan, start and operate businesses. As a serial entrepreneur he has over 20 years of experience having started successful multi-million dollar enterprises. He has founded companies in the health care industry, telecommunications industry, transportation industry and the educational industry. He has over 20 years in the relationship marketing industry and was the Founder and President of a relationship marketing company. He is currently the CEO of Lead Again International, a global management consulting firm specializing in business and leadership development training.

Thomas has been featured in newspapers, magazines and radio programs over the years. He was also featured on the Hallmark Channel television program, *Leadership by the Book* hosted by International Best Selling author Ken Blanchard. As a sought after professional speaker, corporate trainer and servant leader, he shares not only powerful insights on how to be successful in business, he also shares principles on how one can live a life of significance. His passion is to help equip leaders to become the leaders they were created to be. For more information on speaking engagements, to order more books, or to visit his blog, you can log on at: www.leadagain.com.

Disclaimer and Terms of Use

The authors and publisher of this How to Win in Relationship Marketing book and any associated or accompanying materials make no representations or warranties with regards to the completeness, fitness, applicability or accuracy of the content of this book. Every effort was taken to accurately present this product; no guarantees or promises have been made or implied regarding income or any other earnings one may realize as a result of this material. This material is for educational purposes only and any application of the techniques and strategies discussed herein shall be implemented by individual readers at their own discretion and as such readers take full responsibility for associated outcomes.

Information found in this book or the associated web site may contain information that includes or is based upon forward looking statements. Any and all forward looking statements contained in this material or on the web site are intended to express an opinion of its authors but many factors will be important to determine the reader's actual results. The advice of competent legal, tax, accounting or other professionals should be sought.
The authors and publisher do not warrant the performance or applicability of any sites listed or linked to the How to Win in Relationship Marketing book or site. All links are for educational and information purposes. The authors and publisher shall not be held liable to any party for any damages arising out of the use of this material. This material is provided "as is" and is without warranties to any party.

The How to Win in Relationship Marketing book and associated materials are copyrighted by Lead Again International, Inc. No part of this and related material may be changed in any format, copied, sold or used in any way without the expressed written consent of the publisher under any circumstances.